The Monkey Kingdom (Species of Monkeys) 3rd Grade Science Series

Speedy Publishing LLC
40 E. Main St. #1156
Newark, DE 19711
www.speedypublishing.com

There are currently 264 known monkey species.

Pygmy marmosets are the smallest type of monkey. Pygmy marmosets do a lot of climbing because tree sap is their favorite food.

Mandrills mostly live in tropical rainforests. Mandrills have an omnivorous diet consisting mostly of fruits and insects.

The proboscis monkeys are native to the Borneo Island. Proboscis monkeys are omnivores and they primarily feed on leaves and fruits especially unripe fruits.

Japanese macaques are omnivores. Their diet consists of barks, twigs, fruit, insects, eggs and small mammals. Japanese macaques live in large groups called troops.

The White-faced Saki live in monogamous pairs or small family groups. The white-faced saki can be found in Brazil, French Guiana, Guyana, Suriname and Venezuela.

Howler
monkeys are
the loudest of
all monkeys.
These monkeys
live in Central
and South
America.

The yellow baboon has a slim body with long arms and legs and a yellowish-brown hair. Yellow baboons use at least 10 different vocalizations to communicate.

Red-shanked
douc is one
of the most
colourful
primate species.
the red-
shanked douc
spends almost
all of its time
feeding high in
the treetops.

The pied
tamarin is a
small species of
monkey found
in the rainforest
of Brazil. The
pied tamarin
is most active
during the day
and rests in
the safety of
the tree tops
during the night.

The mona
monkey lives
throughout
western Africa.
Mona monkeys
respond to
danger by
freezing
in place.

The mantled guereza is native to much of west central and east Africa. The mantled guereza lives in social groups of three to fifteen individuals.

Gee's golden langur is considered sacred by many Himalayan people. The gee's golden langur can be found in a small region of western Assam, India.

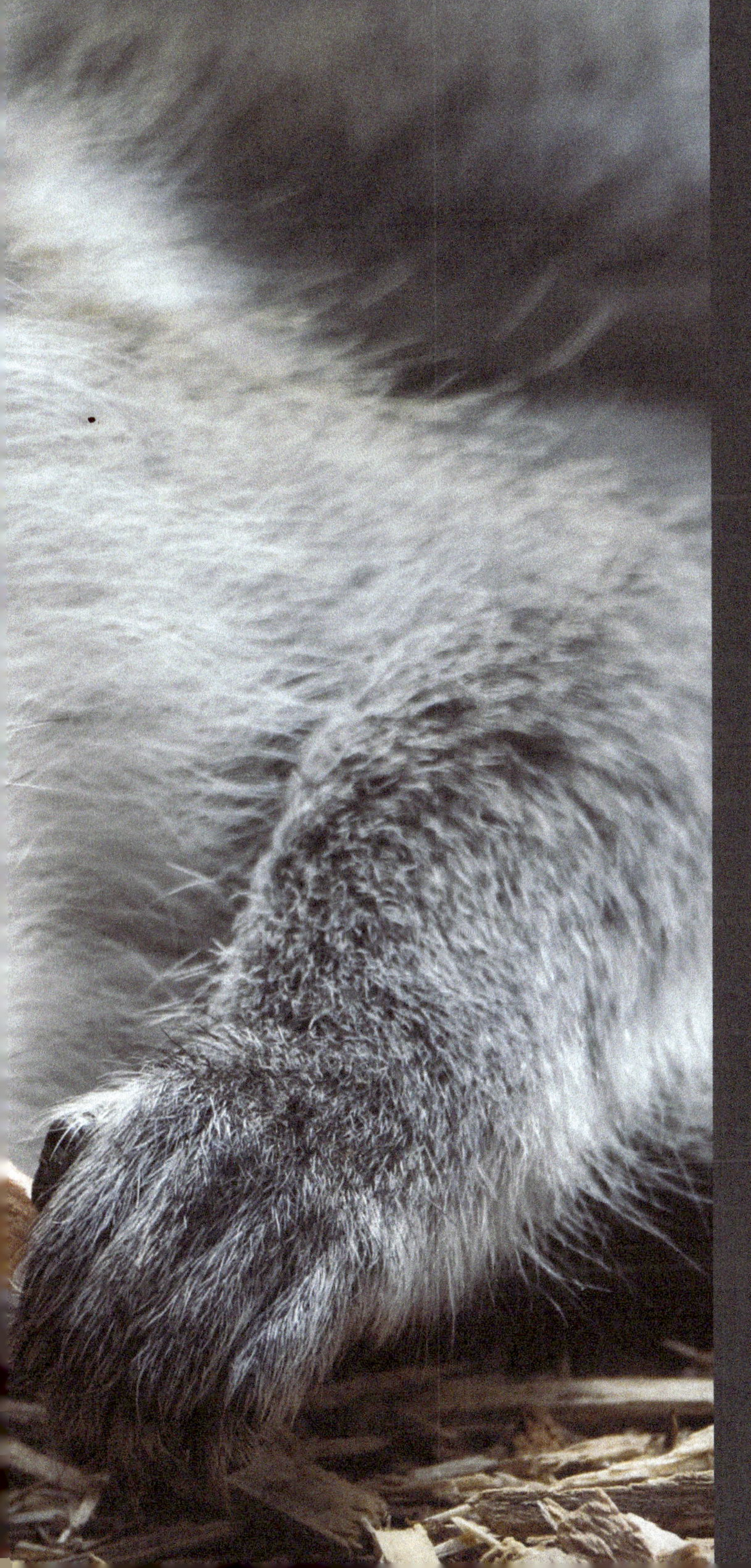

The grivet is most active in the morning and in early evening. Females will have a limited number of mates, while males will have numerous.

The Javan lutung
is found on and
endemic to the
island of Java.
It feeds mainly
on leaves, fruit,
flowers, flower
buds, and
insect larvae.